WHO WAS JESUS?

A little book of guidance

JAMES D. G. DUNN

To St Paul's F3A group
for great fellowship and discussion

First published in Great Britain in 2016

Society for Promoting Christian Knowledge
36 Causton Street
London SW1P 4ST
www.spck.org.uk

Copyright © James D. G. Dunn 2016

British Library Cataloguing-in-Publication Data
A catalogue record for this book is available from the British Library

ISBN 978–0–281–07660–4
eBook ISBN 978–0–281–07661–1

Typeset by Graphicraft Limited, Hong Kong
First printed in Great Britain by Ashford Colour Press
Subsequently digitally printed in Great Britain

eBook by Graphicraft Limited, Hong Kong

Produced on paper from sustainable forests

Contents

About the author

James Dunn is Emeritus Lightfoot Professor of Divinity at Durham University, where he taught from 1982 to 2003. Previously, from 1970 to 1982, he was at the University of Nottingham. He has an MA and BD from the University of Glasgow, his alma mater, and a PhD and DD from the University of Cambridge, and is a Fellow of the British Academy (FBA). He is the author of over twenty monographs, including *Baptism in the Holy Spirit, Jesus and the Spirit, Unity and Diversity in the New Testament, Christology in the Making, The Partings of the Ways, The Theology of Paul the Apostle, The New Perspective on Paul, A New Perspective on Jesus, New Testament Theology: An Introduction, Did the First Christians Worship Jesus?, Jesus, Paul and the Gospels, The Oral Gospel Tradition,* and commentaries on Romans, Galatians, Colossians and Philemon, and Acts. His most recent work is a trilogy tracing the first 150 years of Christianity, *Christianity in the Making.* His doctoral pupils teach in many different parts of the world. He is married to Meta and they have three children. He functioned as a Methodist Local Preacher for forty years. He and his wife have now retired to Chichester to be nearer their daughters and worship at the local parish church.

1

Introduction

Who was Jesus? What a good question. It's a good question because of Jesus' reputation. For nearly two millennia Christians have regarded him as God's Son. That is, not just as *a* son of God, as millions of Christians and others might think of themselves as sons (or daughters) of God. One of the greatest of the earliest Christians, Paul, encouraged his fellow Christians to think of themselves in that way. But Paul is clear that the relationship thus expressed is not ours by nature. He refers to it as a relationship which has come about by adoption (Romans 8.15). The implication is clear. Jesus' sonship was different from that of Christians. As a natural son is different from an adopted son, so, in his relationship with God, Jesus is different from Christians in general.

If Paul, the author of the letter to Rome, probably written in the mid-50s of the first century, is any guide, this conviction about Jesus was already a defining mark of the first Christians. Already, within 30 years of Jesus' death, he was regarded as God's son in a unique sense by the first generation of Christians. Not just as a great leader, cruelly put to death by the Romans. And not just as a messenger who brought a message from God, like the prophets of old. But as unique among human beings.

1

As more closely related to God than earlier saints and prophets. How could this be so? How did this conviction about Jesus come about? Who *was* Jesus?

Sources

To answer these questions satisfactorily we have to know what sources are available to us. The obvious answer is: the Gospels which make up the first four books of the New Testament. The first three, Matthew, Mark and Luke, are very similar. They are usually called the Synoptic Gospels, because they can be 'seen together'. Indeed, they can be set down in three parallel columns, where the degree of overlap becomes immediately evident. The strong majority view is that of these three, Mark is the earliest, and that it served as a primary source for Matthew and Luke.

Specialists in the subject are equally confident that Matthew and Luke were able to use another source, a collection of Jesus' teachings. This latter is usually known as Q, denoting the German word for 'source' (*Quelle*). The size of Q is unclear, since traditions about Jesus and his teaching were no doubt being variously used and circulated. In fact, much of the Q material is evident from the word-for-word agreement between Matthew and Luke. But other shared tradition is quite different in detail, suggesting that Matthew and Luke drew it from different sources.

The principal reason why Mark is regarded as the first of the three New Testament Gospels is simple. It is much more likely, for example, that Matthew added all his teaching material (drawn chiefly from Q) to Mark's briefer account, than that Mark chose to omit so much of the teaching contained in Matthew. Matthew, indeed, seems to have absorbed almost all of Mark. And since Matthew was greatly prized and much used in the second century it is hard to identify distinctive use of Mark's Gospel during that period.

The general view is that Mark was written a little before or a little after the destruction of Jerusalem in AD 70, and that Matthew and Luke were written sometime in the following two decades. The written Q must have been earlier than Matthew and Luke. But, interestingly, the written Q was not preserved. This may be simply because it was totally used by Matthew and Luke, but probably also because it did not take the form of a 'Gospel' in the sense given to that word by Paul and Mark – that is, as an account of Jesus' ministry climaxing in his death and resurrection.

The date of Jesus' death is debated but most settle on AD 30 as the most likely. If so, it means that there was a gap of about 40 years between his ministry and Mark's account. During that time, as can be easily imagined, there must have been an extensive and diverse oral tradition being passed among the spreading churches of earliest Christianity, recalling and narrating Jesus' teaching and ministry. The significance of our being able to set out the first three Gospels in parallel is, not least, that we can clearly see that they were drawing on very similar traditions about Jesus. 'The same, yet different' well describes the Synoptic tradition. The important corollary is that we can gain a very clear picture of Jesus, even when differently portrayed by the first three Evangelists.[1]

This ties in neatly with the early tradition that Mark had been a close companion of Peter (1 Peter 5.13), and the slightly later note of Papias that Mark had acted as Peter's 'interpreter/translator' and had recorded Peter's recollections. Matthew, of course, was one of Jesus' twelve disciples. As a tax collector (Matthew 9.9) he was one of a small minority who could read and write. And as the 'I' passages in Acts indicate, the author of Luke and Acts was a close companion of Paul (also Colossians 4.14). So, in each case, we can be confident that the first three Gospels draw on direct memories of the first generation of Jesus' disciples.

The fourth Gospel in the New Testament is different. The source of its recollections may well be another of Jesus' disciples. But there was more than one 'John' in earliest Christianity, and the tradition is unclear at this point. More important is the fact that John's Gospel was evidently doing something different from the other New Testament Gospels. In particular, the concise teaching of the Synoptics, with many parables, is replaced by lengthy dialogues and disputes with Pharisees,[2] in which Jesus makes amazingly bold 'I am' claims. For example, 'I am the way, and the truth, and the life' (John 14.6). At the same time, a closer examination soon makes clear that most of the dialogues are rooted in the sort of sayings which the Synoptic Evangelists recorded.

The most obvious inference to be drawn is that John was not trying simply to record what Jesus said and did (like the Synoptics). His goal was rather to reflect on and draw out the significance of Jesus for a much wider audience. Thus, for example, the great bread of life discourse in John 6 reads like an extensive reflection on Jesus' words at the Last Supper with his disciples: 'This is my body'; 'This is my blood' (Mark 14.22, 24). And in John 10, Jesus' elaborated claim to be the good shepherd is most simply explained as growing out of Jesus' use of the imagery of sheep (as in Matthew 18.2–3). John gives the impression of being as much concerned to reach out to the future and not just to recall the past.

What of other Gospels? The Gospel of Thomas, only discovered in 1945–6, has roused much speculation and controversy. And it certainly contains what may best be described as Synoptic-like material. But added to that, and clearly intended as the 'good news', is an understanding of the human condition which is best described as 'Gnostic'. The Gnostic gospel worked from a fundamental distinction of flesh and spirit, which is quite different from the teaching of Jesus and the first Christians. More striking still, the Gospel of Thomas has no place for Jesus' death and resurrection. And yet it was precisely the focus on Jesus' death and resurrection which Paul enshrined in the word 'gospel'. And it was Mark who extended this use to an account of Jesus' ministry, climaxing in his death and resurrection. If the New Testament determines what the 'gospel' is, then the four New Testament Evangelists equally determine what a 'Gospel' is.

2

Jesus' life

Son of Mary

Jesus has been a controversial figure for most of the last 2,000 years. Some have even doubted that he ever existed. An easy way to dismiss the central claims of Christianity is to deny that there ever was a historical figure called Jesus. But there is more than a hint of desperation in the promotion of such a view. For Jesus is referred to by Jewish and Roman historians writing of the period with no hint that his existence was questioned by any. His brother James was an important and well-known figure in the early decades of Christianity. There are features of his ministry, for example, that he regularly taught by telling parables, which can hardly be explained as derived from the early church, since no one else was known as such a parabolist. And the earliest written references to his death (and resurrection) can be traced back to within two or three years of that event. So, by far the most obvious reading of the historical data is that there was indeed a man called Jesus who existed in the early decades of the first century.

If we begin at the usual place in writing a biography, or telling the story of an individual, we can say

6

straightforwardly: he was the son of Mary. The birth narratives, only in two of the four New Testament Gospels (Matthew and Luke), may seem rather contrived. And the portrayal of a virgin mother giving birth would certainly raise eyebrows, then as now. But that someone called Mary was his mother is confirmed by other references apart from the birth narratives.[1] So we can take this as one of the firmest facts that we know about Jesus. There are also clear recollections that he had brothers – James, Joses/Joseph, Judas and Simon – and sisters too (Mark 6.3).[2]

Where Jesus was born is more open to question. Of course, Bethlehem, south of Jerusalem, has been acclaimed as the birthplace of Jesus from earliest times, as attested by the traditions recounted in the opening chapters of Matthew and Luke. But there are serious historical questions regarding these traditions. In particular, there is no supporting evidence that the Emperor Augustus decreed a universal census throughout the Roman Empire. So, no obvious reason either for Joseph to have taken his pregnant wife from Galilee to Bethlehem, as Luke narrates (Luke 2.1–5). One cannot but wonder whether the primary root of the story lies in the prophecy of Micah 5.2, that from Bethlehem would come forth 'one who is to rule in Israel'.

The principal clue as to Jesus' date of birth is that it happened 'in the time of king Herod' (Matthew 2.1; Luke 1.5). That will be Herod the Great, who ruled over Judea as a client king of the Roman superpower from 30 to 4 BC. The attribution of 'the slaughter of the innocents' to Herod (Matthew 2.16–18) is otherwise unattested, though it is consistent with his known character. Herod's death (4 BC) presumably means that Jesus' birth can be dated no later than that date.

Jesus of Nazareth

Whatever we make of the birth narratives, we can be quite confident that Jesus was brought up in Nazareth, and was known simply as 'Jesus of Nazareth'. That is how he is referred to from the first, according to the Gospels (e.g. Mark 1.24; John 18.5, 7). And that is how he continued to be identified in the earliest preaching in Acts (e.g. Acts 2.22). Indeed, according to Acts 22.8, it was how Jesus identified himself in the encounter which converted Saul/Paul on the road to Damascus. At that time Nazareth was a small and insignificant village in the south of Galilee. It is not even mentioned in the Old Testament. So there is no reason why Jesus should have been linked with it – that is, no reason other than that was where he was brought up.[3]

The intriguing question of his early life is only heightened by the story of the family's visit to Jerusalem for the Passover festival (Luke 2.41–51). In this story the 12-year-old Jesus is depicted as 'sitting among the teachers' in the Temple, listening to them and asking them questions – as he had been, apparently, for more than three days (2.46). It is difficult to discern whether the story is based on a clear reminiscence, or is a precursor of the fanciful tales told about Jesus in the late second-century Infancy Gospel of Thomas.

Baptized by John

The story of Jesus, however, really begins where the earliest Gospel, Mark, begins – with his being baptized by John the Baptist. Luke tells us that this happened when Jesus was about 30 years old (Luke 3.23), so about 26 CE.

That all four Gospels begin their account of Jesus' ministry with his encounter with John is one of the most striking features of these early reminiscences regarding Jesus. What is most striking is not what John declares about Jesus: that as he (John) baptized with water, so Jesus would baptize with the Holy Spirit (and with fire) (Mark 1.8).[4] It is rather the fact that Jesus is recalled as presenting himself to John to be baptized with 'a baptism of repentance for the forgiveness of sins' (Mark 1.4; Luke 3.3). Both Mark and Matthew note that those who came forward for baptism were baptized 'confessing their sins' (Matthew 3.6; Mark 1.5). Matthew at least, however, was conscious of questions being raised about Jesus accepting a baptism of repentance. So he inserts the additional narrative that the Baptist objected to the idea of Jesus being baptized by him, to which Jesus responds that it was nonetheless fitting thus 'to fulfil all righteousness' (Matthew 3.14–15). The implication presumably is that Jesus saw his baptism as expressing his solidarity with baptized sinners.

Probably implied also is that baptism in water was understood by the first followers of Jesus as the necessary preliminary to or anticipation of the much more desirable baptism in the Spirit. This indeed is what Jesus himself experienced when he emerged from the water of baptism (Mark 1.10–11) and could not unfairly be regarded as in line with what the Baptist had predicted. The relation of the two baptisms (water and Spirit) remains one of the most unclear and indeed contested issues in the history of Christianity.

What followed from Jesus' baptism is also somewhat confused and confusing. The first three (Synoptic) Gospels all recount Jesus immediately being subjected to temptation in the wilderness for 40 days – Matthew and Luke with some detail (Matthew 4.1–11; Luke 4.1–13). But not the Fourth Gospel. Thereafter Matthew and Mark report that Jesus went (back) to Galilee, 'after John [the Baptist] was arrested' (Mark 1.14; Matthew 4.12). The Fourth Evangelist, however, has Jesus moving back and forward from Judea to Galilee and again to Judea (John 1.43, 2.13). During this period the Baptist was still ministering, and Jesus' disciples are recalled as also baptizing (3.22), though John adds, Jesus himself did not baptize (4.2). This would seem to recall an early period when Jesus modelled his own ministry to some extent on the Baptist's, and would probably explain why the other Evangelists ignored this period. The implication is probably that Jesus' distinctive ministry only began when he had left the near company of the Baptist and began his own mission in his home territory. Does that also imply that Jesus did not gain a clear idea of what his mission should be, as distinct from that of the Baptist, for some time following his baptism?

Ministry in Galilee

It should probably occasion no surprise that in giving their account of Jesus, Matthew, Mark and Luke focused their attention on his ministry in Galilee, and held back his going south to Jerusalem to serve as the climax of his mission. Why they did so is hardly clear. But it would appear that the Fourth Evangelist was able to pull out (and elaborate) various reminiscences of Jesus in Judea/Jerusalem prior to his final week which the other Evangelists had ignored, for whatever reason. In contrast, after the opening chapters, John limits his record of Jesus' ministry in Galilee to his account of the feeding of the 5,000 (6.1–14), typically with an extensive sequence of teaching attached (6.25–65). The fact that the two accounts of Jesus' mission (Synoptic and Johannine) are so different – the former full of parables and epigrammatic sayings, the latter containing extensive discourses and discussions – suggests, as already noted, that the Synoptic accounts well represent

Jesus' teaching style in Galilee, whereas the Fourth Gospel's account is the product of some lengthy reflection on Jesus, and on the significance of what he said and did.

According to the Synoptic accounts Jesus made his base in Capernaum, on the northern side of the Sea of Galilee. His first disciples were Galilean fishermen, the brothers, Simon Peter and Andrew, James and John (Mark 1.16–20), and his mission was mainly round that large lake. Many of his parables and the images used in his teaching reflect these settings. Most of the healings and exorcisms attributed to him took place in this region. He is also recorded as making occasional visits to the region of Tyre, north-west of Galilee (7.24), and to Decapolis, the eastern side of the river Jordan (5.20; 7.31). But Galilee and its lake was evidently the principal focus of his mission. Was this a deliberate way of his keeping out of trouble from the high priestly and Pharisaic factions centred in Jerusalem? Perhaps. It may be significant that Luke records a number of positive interactions with Pharisees during that period (Luke 7.36; 11.37; 14.1). But the implication is clear that Jesus gained a considerable degree of support from and for his Galilean mission, which probably set alarm bells ringing in Jerusalem. The Fourth Evangelist even recalls a wave of enthusiasm to make Jesus king, a move from which Jesus shied away (John 6.15).

The way to Jerusalem

When the conviction became compelling for Jesus that he must go to Jerusalem, as the climax of his mission, is not at all clear. The question, of course, is confused by the Fourth Gospel's focus on early visits to and time spent in and around Jerusalem. But Mark seems to have constructed his Gospel to build up to a climactic event in the north of Galilee, recalled as the 'Transfiguration'. In this event Jesus is remembered as being joined by Moses and Elijah on a mountain top, witnessed by Peter, James and John (Mark 9.2–8). How much was their recollection and how much a figurative telling, both of a growing realization of how significant Jesus was and of a growing anticipation of what was to come, we can no longer determine. But Mark certainly presents it and Peter's preceding confession that Jesus was the Messiah (8.27–29) as a turning point.[5] It is from this point that Mark records Jesus as predicting his rejection, death and resurrection (8.31; 9.31; 10.33–34), an unexpected fate for the hoped-for Messiah. And Luke dates Jesus' determination to go to Jerusalem more or less from that time (Luke 9.51; cf. Mark 10.32–33).

The climax of the journey to Jerusalem was the arrangement which Jesus evidently contrived that he should ride into Jerusalem on an unbroken colt (Mark 11.1–11). According to Mark it was set up as a triumphal entry with the crowd hailing 'the one who comes in the name of the Lord' (11.9). How contrived it was is not clear, though the consistency with the enthusiasm shown in Galilee is probably significant. Was Jesus, then, playing to the crowd, or seeking to arouse their support, in anticipation of hostility from the leading Temple authorities? The fact that no allusion is made back to the 'triumphal entry' in what follows may not be significant. For what followed, the next day, must have been the much greater provocation – traditionally known as 'the cleansing of the Temple' (11.15–17). This was when Jesus drove out the buyers and sellers of animals sold in the Temple courts for sacrifice, and overturned the tables of those who changed the money of worshippers for the currency necessary to buy the sacrificial animals. The Fourth Evangelist chose to put this event at the front of his Gospel (John 2.13–22), presumably as providing a key event symbolic for the readers of/listeners to his Gospel. But the Synoptic timing is quite firm. And it is no surprise that the Temple authorities should regard this as the last straw and should decide that Jesus had to be put away. The fact that they held back because the crowd was 'spellbound by his teaching' (Mark 11.18) also has an authentic ring and explains why they did not act against Jesus immediately.

Jesus' betrayal, trial and execution

Jesus evidently did not shy away from the likelihood that the Jerusalem authorities would act against him, though Mark notes that he made a point of sleeping in Bethany, a short distance from the city (11.11–12, 19; 14.3). However, the implication is that the breadth of support for him, presumably principally from those coming to the Passover celebration from Galilee, was sufficient to make the authorities hesitate before doing anything. The problem was resolved, evidently, by the decision of one of Jesus' own immediate disciples, Judas Iscariot, to engineer an occasion when he could betray Jesus to the authorities. Why he did so is not made clear – possibly as a way of forcing Jesus to declare his hand, to make clear his claims and aims in defiance of the Jerusalem authorities, both Jewish and Roman, in which case the assumption presumably would have been that the support of pilgrims would have been strong enough to ensure success. The Evangelists naturally show no sympathy towards Judas. He is referred to simply as 'Jesus' betrayer'.[6] The Fourth Gospel adds that he kept the disciples' common purse and used to steal from it (John 12.6). Matthew records his repentance after the Jewish court condemned Jesus and his despairing suicide (Matthew 27.3–5). And Luke presumably takes some satisfaction in describing his more horrific end (Acts 1.18–20).

The principal story line is that having moved freely between Jerusalem and Bethany for several days after his entry, Jesus had contrived a special gathering of his immediate followers in the city, in which he celebrated a Passover meal with them. The timing is unclear, whether it was the actual Passover day or just before (note John 19.14). What has mattered for Christians ever since is that at this meal (on the Thursday evening) Jesus instituted the Last Supper. This was when he instructed his disciples to regard the bread and wine he was giving them to eat and drink as his body and blood (Mark 14.22–24). The breaking of the bread and drinking of the wine was recalled by the first Christians as the establishment of a new covenant with God (1 Corinthians 11.23–26). The fact that the Fourth Gospel does not describe the Last Supper as such leaves it unclear as to whether Judas participated in the Supper or left before Jesus had instituted it (John 13.26–30).

The other Gospels indicate Jesus' expectation of betrayal (Mark 14.17–21), and the very fact that he went out of the city only so far as nearby Gethsemane suggests that Jesus was well aware of what was afoot. His prayer in Gethsemane and his disciples' obliviousness to what was about to happen is one of the most heart-rending episodes in the Gospels (Mark 14.32–42). His arrest and his disciples' abandonment of him are equally traumatic (Mark 14.43–50). Mark records that in the trial which followed, an exceptional gathering of the council, presided over by the High Priest,[7] could make no progress since the testimony against Jesus was confused (14.55–59). It was only when Jesus accepted the title of Messiah – though only Mark has it as a positive affirmation of Jesus himself (14.62) – that the High Priest concluded that he had heard enough to find Jesus guilty of blasphemy and the court condemned him as deserving of death (14.64).

Since the Jewish court did not have power to execute the death penalty, it was necessary to pass Jesus over for trial by the Roman governor, Pilate. Luke recalls Pilate as not knowing what to make of the whole business (Luke 23.4) and as passing the buck to Herod Antipas, client king in Galilee, in Jerusalem for the Passover (23.7). The ploy was unsuccessful, though ironically it apparently restored a more positive relation between Pilate and Herod (23.12). Luke indicates that Pilate was willing to release Jesus (23.16), but that he caved in before the continuing demands of the chief priests. Rather extraordinarily, Pilate gave the crowd a choice between Jesus and the much more dangerous Barabbas, who was already in prison 'for an insurrection that had taken place in the city and for murder' (23.19). But this further ploy was also unsuccessful since, presumably to Pilate's surprise, the crowd called for Barabbas rather than Jesus to be released, and for Jesus to be crucified (Mark 15.11–14) – his Galilean supporters either absent or cowed. Pilate complied and Jesus was handed over to be scourged and crucified.

This central act for Christianity, the cross and the crucifixion, is depicted and narrated in some detail and with full poignancy. Today the full horrific reality of crucifixion, following a scourging, is hard even to begin to imagine. One of the last cries of Jesus on the cross was even more heart-rending than the Gethsemane episode: 'Eloi, Eloi, lama sabachthani?', 'My God, my God, why have you forsaken me?' (Mark 15.34). It should occasion no surprise that Jesus died soon after, before those crucified alongside him. The Fourth Evangelist notes that when the decision was made to break the legs of the crucified, to hasten their death, his early death made it unnecessary in Jesus' case – thus fulfilling the stipulations regarding the Passover lamb.[8]

Thus ends the story of Jesus' life. But the story does not end there!

3

Jesus' mission

There are several distinctive features in the Gospels'
accounts of Jesus' mission. We will note, first, the most
striking, in their degree of uniqueness in relation to a
first-century Jewish mission and to its corollaries.

The kingdom of God

This is one of the most characteristic – but also one
of the most distinctive – features of Jesus' preaching.
When the number of references are counted, and allow-
ing for different accounts of the same episodes, Jesus
is remembered as speaking about the kingdom of
God (Matthew prefers 'kingdom of heaven') more than
50 times. Mark begins his account of Jesus' ministry with
the summarized message: 'The time is fulfilled, and the
kingdom of God has come near; repent, and believe
in the good news' (Mark 1.15). 'Good news/gospel' is
Mark's word added here, as he does at other points,[1]
but it sums up his understanding that Jesus' preaching
of the kingdom of God was the heart of his gospel. That
God is king over all the earth was a familiar theme
in Israel's psalm book.[2] 'The Lord reigns' was a familiar

acclamation in Jewish worship.[3] The very fact, then, that Jesus made this theme so central to his preaching and teaching is a stark reminder of how deeply rooted in Israel's Scriptures was Jesus' whole ministry. But it is what Jesus did with it which marks out his message as so distinctive.

To express confidence in the future as in God's hands was in itself not so distinctive. The prayer which Jesus taught his disciples, including the second petition, 'May your kingdom come' (Matthew 6.10/Luke 11.2), seems to have been modelled on an early form of the Jewish Kaddish prayer – 'May he (God) let his kingdom rule in your lifetime . . . speedily and soon.' Even so, however, Jesus' proclamation of the kingdom as having come near suggests a sense that God's intervention on behalf of his people was close at hand. Most noticeably Jesus is recalled as asserting that some of his disciples would 'not taste death until they see that the kingdom of God has come with power' (Mark 9.1). Similarly it is hardly accidental that the first of the Beatitudes attributed to Jesus is 'Blessed are you who are poor, for yours is the kingdom of God' (Luke 6.20/Matthew 5.3). This theme of the kingdom of God implying a reversal of typical values and expectations was evidently a feature of Jesus' message. The kingdom belongs to those who are like little children (Mark 10.14–15). Toll-collectors and prostitutes would enter the kingdom of God before many of those who heard Jesus (Matthew 21.31).

More striking still, however, would have been Jesus' affirmation that the kingdom had already come, or was already active in the present. Most notably Jesus is recalled as affirming in regard to his exorcisms: 'If it is by the finger/Spirit of God that I cast out demons, then the kingdom of God has come to you' (Matthew 12.28/Luke 11.20). The similar theme of longed-for expectations realized in what Jesus was doing appears in several other passages. His presence is like that of a bridegroom at his wedding, like new cloth or new wine (Mark 2.18–22). He answers the doubting query from the imprisoned Baptist by pointing to how many of Isaiah's expectations regarding the hoped-for future are being realized in his ministry (Matthew 11.2–6/Luke 7.18–23). He does not hesitate to claim that 'something greater than Jonah', 'something greater than Solomon' is here (Matthew 12.41–42/Luke 11.31–32). What was happening now, through his ministry, is what many prophets and righteous/kings had longed to see (Matthew 13.17/Luke 10.24).

The importance of God's kingdom in Jesus' preaching is all the more striking, since it is not clear how his disciples responded to it. Certainly talk of the kingdom was not so prominent among his followers after Jesus. And the theme of its presence in and through Jesus' ministry is in effect replaced in early Christian preaching by proclamation of Jesus' death and resurrection. It is true that in his account of Christianity's beginnings Luke does retain an emphasis on the kingdom of God[4] – but he also hints that the message was easily misunderstood (Acts 1.6). And compared with Jesus, Paul makes relatively little reference to the kingdom of God. Indeed, apart from John 3.3, 5 and 18.36, John, in his account of Jesus' life and ministry, ignores the theme altogether. It is all the more striking, then, that Matthew, Mark and Luke have retained so fully the memory of Jesus focusing so much on this theme and expressing the rule of God in his own ministry. But should we detect an uneasiness on the part of (some of) his first followers, not least in the light of Jesus' execution, that continued emphasis on Jesus as embodying or exercising kingly power was deemed too dangerously political?

Teller of parables

Another striking and distinctive feature of Jesus' ministry was that he conveyed so much of his message by telling parables. He is recalled as telling more than 40 stories, and using them to teach with great effect. That no one else in the beginnings of Christianity has a similar or even a nearly similar reputation can only mean that this too was a characteristic feature of Jesus' mission. The fact is noteworthy in itself, since the characteristic of his parables is that their effect is often immediate – the stories themselves catch the attention – and their point is all the more effective after a little reflection or the self-examination which they so often demand. Apart from the Lord's Prayer, nothing of Jesus' teaching is so widely familiar as several of his parables – the Sower (Mark 4.1–9, 13–20), the Wicked Tenants (Mark 12.1–12), the Talents and Pounds (Matthew 25.14–30/Luke 19.11–27), the Wheat and Weeds (Matthew 13.24–30, 13.36–43), the Labourers in the Vineyard (Matthew 20.1–16), the Wise and Foolish Bridesmaids (Matthew 25.1–13), the Judgment of Sheep and Goats (Matthew 25.31–46), the Good Samaritan (Luke 10.25–37), the Rich Fool (Luke 12.13–21), the Lost Sheep, the Lost Coin and the Lost Son (Luke 15), the Rich Man and Lazarus (Luke 16.19–31), the Unjust Judge (Luke 18.1–8), and the Pharisee and the Tax Collector (Luke 18.9–14).

That Jesus told so many brief stories to convey his teaching is striking in itself. Indeed, parables were so characteristic of Jesus' teaching that according to Mark 'he did not speak to them except in parables' (Mark 4.34). Mark, followed by Matthew and Luke, also reports that Jesus reflected on the effectiveness and ineffectiveness of parables (Mark 4.11–12). For these stories only 'work' when they engage the listeners. And the fact that so many of them have been preserved, when no one else tried to rely on such a means of teaching, strongly suggests that they worked very effectively in recruiting disciples and in training them to see what really mattered in Jesus' teaching and in their discipleship. That they cannot simply be transformed into prose teaching means that they continued to involve Jesus' followers by in effect continuing to require them to discern what their priorities should be.

As such a distinctive and engaging feature of Jesus' ministry they tell us much about how he attracted so many to his ministry – and infuriated others!

Concern for the poor

Another striking feature of Jesus' mission was his concern for the poor. Such a concern, of course, is rooted in the Jewish law's own provision for the poor.[5] It is nonetheless notable that when his teachings were gathered together, it is the Beatitudes which come first, and the first Beatitude is the declaration that it is the poor who are blessed and who are assured the kingdom of God is theirs. Matthew somewhat spiritualizes the blessing: it is 'the poor in spirit' who are declared blessed (Matthew 5.3). But the Lukan parallel suggests that Jesus' primary thought was for the (physically) poor (Luke 6.20). This is probably confirmed by the fact that Luke records the second benediction as bestowed on 'you who are hungry now' (Luke 6.21), whereas the Matthean equivalent is a benediction on 'those who hunger and thirst for righteousness' (Matthew 5.6). Why Matthew should so spiritualize Jesus' Beatitudes is not clear, especially as he retains unchanged the report of Jesus' response to the Baptist's doubting query by referring him to the fulfilment of Isaiah's expectations in his mission: 'Go and tell John what you hear and see: the blind receive their sight, the lame walk, the lepers are cleansed, the deaf hear, the dead are raised, and (the climactic point) the poor have good news brought to them' (Matthew 11.4–5/Luke 7.22).

That responsibility towards and good news for the poor were integral features of Jesus' mission is confirmed by other passages in the Gospels. All three Synoptics highlight the account of the rich young man who deeply impressed Jesus by his piety, but who lacked one thing – willingness to sell his possessions and give to the poor (Mark 10.17–22). All three Synoptists attached (or retained) the teaching which follows in their narratives: that it is easier for a camel to go through the eye of a needle than for a rich man to enter the kingdom of God (Mark 10.25). Mark and Luke also record Jesus' commendation of the poor widow who in putting into the offering 'two small copper coins' had 'put in all she had to live on' (Mark 12.41–44/Luke 21.1–4). And Luke makes a point of recording Jesus in the Nazareth synagogue reading the first words of Isaiah 61, 'The Spirit of the Lord is upon me, because he has anointed me to bring good news to the poor' (Luke 4.18). It is a striking feature of Luke's account that he gives so much attention to this aspect of Jesus' mission. He records Jesus as encouraging a leading Pharisee to invite the poor, the crippled, the lame and the blind to his banquets (14.13, 21). It is Luke who retains the parable of the Rich Man and Lazarus (16.19–31). And only Luke records the story of the chief tax collector, Zacchaeus, who in response to Jesus' readiness to come to his house, promises to give half of his goods to the poor (19.8). To which Jesus responds by affirming that 'Today salvation has come to this house' (19.9).

It is presumably from the precedent set by the Scriptures and emphasized by Jesus that Paul and the first Christians gave such precedence to making provision for the poor.[6] Somewhat surprisingly, Luke never mentions the 'poor' in the sequel to his Gospel (the Acts of the Apostles), though the concern is otherwise indicated (Acts 6.1–6). So the emphasis on the priority of the poor which is such a prominent feature of his Gospel was presumably not Luke's but a genuine recollection of what Jesus himself counted as important.

Exorcist and healer

Jesus' response to the Baptist's query, already cited (Matthew 11.5–6/Luke 7.22), clearly indicates how importantly Jesus regarded the healings which are remembered as such a major part of his ministry. The allusions to Isaiah's expectations of the day when hopes would be realized – the blind seeing, the lame walking, the deaf hearing[7] – clearly indicate Jesus' own perception of the significance of this aspect of his mission. Similarly the Q collection of Jesus' teaching has put together sayings of Jesus on the significance of his exorcisms (Matthew12.25–30/Luke 11.17–23). In response to criticisms, that 'by the ruler of the demons he cast out demons' (Mark 3.22), Jesus is recalled as pointing out that such a charge could be equally levelled against other exorcists who had operated acceptably in Israel. More significantly, he continues: 'But if it is by the Spirit/finger of God that I cast out demons, then the kingdom of God has come to you.'

It is not necessary to go into the question of the historicity of each of the healings and miracles attributed to Jesus. So far as exorcisms are concerned, it is sufficiently clear that many ailments and conditions were attributed to evil forces, and that Jesus acted on the same general assumption. What also remains clear is that Jesus was remembered as someone who exercised an effective ministry of healing and restoration. Exorcisms indeed were recalled as a regular and common feature of his ministry in Galilee.[8] Mark similarly focuses the commissioning of Jesus' twelve disciples on their being sent out 'to preach and to have authority to cast out demons' (Mark 3.14–15; 6.7, 13). And the exorcising of the Gerasene demoniac and of the epileptic boy are two of the most prominent of Mark's accounts of Jesus' ministry (5.1–20; 9.14–29). Demons or unclean spirits are not referred to very often in the rest of the NT, though in Acts 10.38 Peter's sermon to the Roman centurion Cornelius recalls Jesus' ministry as 'doing good and healing all who were oppressed by the devil'. And Jesus' disciples are recalled as successfully invoking his name in their own ministry of exorcism (Luke 10.17; Acts 16.18). So in terms of the understanding of the day Jesus was widely regarded as a very effective exorcist.

The self-testimony of Matthew 11.5/Luke 7.22 includes reference to various healings. It is clear that Jesus' reputation as a healer went well beyond his success as an exorcist – though since illness would often have been attributed to demonic influence there is no clear distinction at this point. The healings attributed to him are extensive, as Peter's sermon to Cornelius implies (Acts 10.38). He is recalled as healing blindness with a touch.[9] Similarly he healed lepers with touch or a word (Mark 1.40–45; Luke 17.11–19). His touch was remembered as often effective,[10] most striking in the case of a woman with a haemorrhage (Mark 5.25–34). At other times a word from Jesus was sufficient (Mark 2.1–12; 3.1–6), remarkably in one case at least at a distance (Matthew 8.5–13/Luke 7.1–10). He is even recalled as raising the dead, in the case of Jairus's daughter (Mark 5.35–43; Luke 7.11–17).

Since medical knowledge was so limited at that time, and indeed only became more extensive and better grounded in comparatively recent times, it is hardly possible to achieve a clear impression of either need or effect in the cases listed above. The fact that in the earliest days of Christianity similar claims to effective healings were made[11] should be enough to indicate that healings did happen, and that Jesus' reputation as a healer and exorcist was well deserved. Not least of significance is the fact that healings and exorcisms were performed 'in the name of Jesus Christ'.[12] The clear implication is that his reputation as a healer gave his name an effective authority even when used by others (Mark 9.38–39).

Harder to get their heads round for people today are the accounts of what are most conveniently referred to as 'nature miracles'. These include a large catch of fish (Luke 5.1–11; John 21.4–14), stilling a storm (Mark 4.35–41), feeding a multitude (Mark 6.32–44), walking on the sea (Mark 6.45–52) and the withering of a fig tree (Mark 11.12–14). What the memories were behind these stories is inevitably a matter of speculation. Even if we accept an openness then to the possibility of such miracles far in excess of what people today might envisage, the attempts to pick out 'what really happened' as lying behind the current narratives are so speculative and without sound roots as to be virtually a waste of time. What remains and is probably most important is that such miracles were attributed to Jesus, and as early as we can penetrate back historically. His reputation as a healer and miracle worker seems to have been widespread, the only question being what was the source of his authority and power (Mark 3.22–27). That is, Jesus must have made such an impact on his disciples in particular, but also more widely, that there was no doubt among either followers or opponents that he performed such amazing deeds.

The Fourth Evangelist's account raises more questions than it answers. That he made a practice of linking the miracles or signs which he records with lengthy speeches or speech-dialogues is clear. Some of the miracles he records are drawn from the same traditions as the Synoptic accounts – notably the feeding of the 5,000 and the walking on the water (John 6.1–21). But his miracle stories begin and end with two accounts which are otherwise elsewhere unattested in the earliest traditions regarding Jesus – turning water into wine (2.1–11) and raising Lazarus from the dead (11.1–44). That the latter provides the trigger for decisive action against Jesus (11.45–53), rather than the cleansing of the Temple, as in the Synoptics, suggests that in John's retelling of the story symbolism has been given more weight than historical recollection.

Good news for sinners

In many ways this must have been one of the most, if not the most, striking feature of Jesus' mission. For sinners were, by definition, in default. They had ignored or broken the very rules of behaviour which Scripture laid down as essential for acceptance by God and for individuals and people to remain in good standing with God. The Ten Commandments laid down the core requirements made by God, as Jesus also implied (Mark 10.19). And that sinners, those in breach or disregard of these demands, are to be condemned is the universal assumption of Israel's Scriptures.[13] Understandably, then, fundamental to Israel's religion was the provision of a sin offering to cancel out the negative effects of the sin (e.g. Leviticus 4—6).

This being the case, the most striking feature of John the Baptist's mission was that he offered 'a baptism of repentance for the forgiveness of sins' (Mark 1.4). The astonishing and notable feature was that he evidently regarded his baptism as sufficient reassurance to those who responded, that their sins were forgiven. That is, he seemed to bypass and treat as irrelevant the role of priest and sacrifice in the process of cancelling the sin before God. In accepting John's baptism, Jesus presumably accepted or gave consent to the implication that sins could be wiped out/forgiven directly and without priestly intermediation. That this is the appropriate inference is confirmed by the accounts of Jesus' own ministry which follow.

What appears to be one of the earliest memories of Jesus' mission was his declaration to a paralyzed man, let down through the roof of the house where Jesus was teaching, that his sins were forgiven (Mark 2.5). That these words would have been offensive to those most concerned with the practice of religion is obvious (2.6–7): this was not how sins were to be declared forgiven! Most astonishing, Jesus' response was to the effect that the Son of Man – that is, he himself[14] – had authority on earth (from God) to forgive sins. And, according to the story, he demonstrated this authorization by there and then healing the paralyzed man (2.9–12).

Again, according to Matthew, Mark and Luke, one of the earliest complaints against Jesus was that he ate with sinners and tax collectors (Mark 2.16). To which Jesus replied, somewhat outrageously for the devoutly religious, 'Those who are well have no need of a physician, but those who are sick; I have come to call not the righteous but sinners' (Mark 2.17). To avoid obvious criticism, Luke adds: '. . . sinners to repentance' (Luke 5.32). Later on he records an occasion when, at a meal hosted by a Pharisee, a woman anointed Jesus with oil, to which Jesus responded by declaring her many sins forgiven – arousing the indignation of other guests (Luke 7.36–50).

Matthew and Luke also recall the dismissive criticism levelled against Jesus: 'a glutton and a drunkard, a friend of tax collectors and sinners' (Matt. 11.19/Luke 7.34). And Luke prefaces his recounting of the parables of the Lost Sheep, Coin and Son by noting that tax collectors and sinners were crowding in upon Jesus, inciting the criticism of Pharisees and scribes that 'This man welcomes sinners and eats with them' (Luke 15.1–2).

Luke also has the risen Jesus commissioning his disciples to preach repentance and forgiveness in his name to all nations (Luke 24.47). And it would certainly appear that this was integral to the message with which the Christian movement began.[15] That this was linked to Jesus' death, seen as fulfilling the function of a sin offering, should not occasion surprise.[16] That Jesus' death thus ended the need for future sin-offerings and for the role of priests to offer such sacrifices was a somewhat unexpected but wholly understandable deduction for the writer of Hebrews to draw. But it certainly underlines the degree to which earliest Christianity found its key to salvation in the death (and resurrection) of Jesus.

The reconstitution of Israel

The 'great commission' at the end of Matthew's Gospel (Matthew 28.18–20), and the expansion of the new movement under the leadership of Paul in particular, make it easy to forget both that Jesus and his first disciples were all Jews, and the extent to which he saw his mission as fulfilling God's plans for his people Israel. For example, his call to repentance echoed the repeated call of Jeremiah to 'Return, faithless Israel/children' (Jeremiah 3.12, 14, 22). His choice of twelve close disciples was presumably intended to echo and indeed model to some extent what Israel should be.[17] His parable of the Lost Sheep (Matthew 18.12/Luke 15.4) and his commission that his disciples should go to 'the lost sheep of the house of Israel' (Matthew 10.6; 15.24) echo the popular Hebrew Bible image of Israel as the flock of Yahweh.[18] His reference to the Last Supper as a 'new covenant' meal (Luke 22.20/1 Corinthians 11.25) clearly echoes Jeremiah's promise of a new covenant with his people (Jeremiah 31.31–34).

The fact that Matthew recalls Jesus' commission to his disciples as restricted to Israel ('Go nowhere among the Gentiles, and enter no town of the Samaritans' – Matthew 10.5) is presumably rooted in an early memory of Jesus' mission. Was this a first stage in Jesus' concept of his mission or just in his mission strategy? We should not forget the extent to which Matthew also makes a point of emphasizing that Jesus' perspective and hope was by no means confined to Israel.[19] That Jesus responded positively to Gentiles calling for help is also clearly recalled.[20] But the questions, whether Jesus' first disciples thought only of a prophetic mission to call Israel to repentance and faith, and whether the extent to which a turn to the Gentiles was primarily the outworking and consequence of Paul's mission, are not so easily resolved.

Here it is probably appropriate to remember that Jesus must have been seen to constitute a challenge or even a threat to Israel's central self-identity. We have already noted that his dealing with 'sinners' was in effect an undermining of the role of priest and sacrifice so central to Israel's religion. Also to be noted is the degree to which he effectively relaxed, or better refocused, the laws of clean and unclean; Mark expresses the teaching in radical terms (Mark 7.1–23; note 7.19b), Matthew more conservatively (Matthew 15.1–20). And John does not hesitate to interpret Jesus' cleansing of the Temple as signifying its replacement by Jesus himself (John 2.19–22). Did such a redefining of central elements of Israel's religion make it inevitable that the movement which Jesus inaugurated would become something different? Was Jesus in effect challenging the distinctive Jewishness of Israel's religion? At the very least the tension between Matthew 10.6, 15.24 and what became Christianity is not so serious as these verses considered on their own might suggest. The story continues in 1 Corinthians 8—10 and Romans 14.1—15.13.

Lukan emphases

The last section naturally included consideration of Matthean emphases in his representation of the Jesus tradition. But the distinctive features in Luke's portrayal of Jesus also deserve some attention. These include the repeated and distinctive references to Jesus praying,[21] as also his equally distinctive emphasis on Jesus as inspired and empowered by the Spirit of God (1.15; 4.1, 18; 10.21). In addition, it is Luke who gives special attention to Jesus' concern for the poor[22] and recalls Jesus' warnings against the perils of wealth.[23] And it is Luke who emphasizes the role of women in supporting Jesus' ministry and Jesus' concern for mothers.[24]

In short, Jesus clearly made a huge and varied impact on his disciples and on those who were attracted and challenged by the Jesus tradition. Luke is a very good example of how varied was the impression which Jesus made.

4

Jesus' self-understanding

Even more intriguing than Jesus' understanding of his mission is his understanding of himself. Why did he go about this mission? What role did he see himself as performing or fulfilling?

His baptismal commission

As already noted, Jesus' acceptance of a baptism of repentance by John was an event most unlikely to have been created by the Jesus tradition. So although the event was likely to be viewed through the spectacles of subsequent faith we can be sufficiently confident in the basic account. This is that as he emerged from the baptismal water Jesus 'saw the heavens torn apart and the Spirit descending like a dove on him. And a voice came from heaven, "You are my Son, the Beloved; with you I am well pleased"' (Mark 1.10–11). Mark implies that it was a very personal vision and experience for Jesus. So how public it was is hardly clear, and we have to assume that Jesus referred to it in talking with his disciples or that they deduced the words of the heavenly voice from what he said or how he acted subsequently.

The words of the heavenly voice are usually deduced as drawing on Psalm 2.7 ('He said to me, "You are my son; today I have begotten you"'), and Isaiah 42.1 ('Here is my servant, whom I uphold, my chosen, in whom my soul delights; I have put my spirit upon him; he will bring forth justice to the nations'). In which case they go a long way towards explaining Jesus' self-consciousness, as we shall see below. Was this the point at which the followers of Jesus believed he in effect became God's son? The subsequent distinction between Jesus as uniquely God's son, and believers as adopted sons (Romans 8.14–17; Galatians 4.4–6) may not have been initially pressed – as the further use of Psalm 2.7 may imply (Acts 13.33; Hebrews 1.5; 5.5). What is probably more important is that the naming of Jesus as God's son was understood to have been accompanied by the Spirit of God coming upon Jesus and in effect anointing him for his subsequent ministry. This presumably explains why the link between sonship and Spirit was so firm from the first – the Spirit prompting in believers the cry 'Abba! Father!' (Romans 8.15; Galatians 4.6). The tradition that Spirit and sonship went together, is evidently rooted in Jesus' own baptismal experience.

That the experience of Jesus at the Jordan also functioned as Jesus' commission is not explicitly stated. But it is clearly implied in the fact that all the Gospels begin Jesus' ministry with his encounter with John. Preparation for ministry is also implied in the Synoptic account of Jesus going into the wilderness 'immediately' (Mark 1.12) after his baptism, and at the prompting of the same Spirit (Mark 1.12) – presumably to reflect on and prepare for what he was being called to do. Luke also notes that Jesus' return from the wilderness to minister in Galilee was at the instigation and empowering of the same Spirit (Luke 4.14).

His sense of commission

Two phrases to describe Jesus' sense of commission appear quite regularly in the Synoptic tradition – 'I came' and 'I was sent.' 'I have come not to call the righteous but sinners' (Mark 2.17). 'The Son of Man came not to be served but to serve, and to give his life a ransom for many' (Mark 10.45). And the more dolorous: 'Do not think that I have come to bring peace to the earth; I have not come to bring peace, but a sword. For I have come to set a man against his father, and a daughter against her mother . . .' (Matthew 10.34–35/Luke 12.51). 'I came to bring fire to the earth, and how I wish it were already kindled!' (Luke 12.49). Clearly comes to expression here a sense of destiny and foreboding.

Similarly Jesus is remembered as speaking on a number of occasions of his sense of commission – 'I was sent.' 'Whoever welcomes me welcomes not me but him who sent me' (Mark 9.37). Matthew recalls a similar saying of Jesus when he sent out his disciples in furtherance of his own mission: 'Whoever welcomes you welcomes me, and whoever welcomes me welcomes the one who sent me' (Matthew 10.40). And Luke records several statements made by Jesus to the same effect.[1]

It is not so important to clarify whether that conviction as to his calling first emerged at Jesus' baptism in the river Jordan. What is important is that such a conviction was a driving force behind Jesus' mission.

A prophet

Understandably, given the role of prophets in Israel's history, the coming of a prophet was part of Israel's hope for the future (Deuteronomy 18.15, 18). It is not surprising, then, that John the Baptist was widely regarded as a prophet, a role which, according to Luke 1.76, his father had prophetically affirmed. This was a role and status of the Baptist which Jesus gladly affirmed – 'a prophet? Yes, I tell you, and more than a prophet' (Matthew 11.9/Luke 7.26). The opinion that John was a prophet was evidently widely shared.[2]

So it is hardly surprising that Jesus should have been regarded in the same terms. Matthew reports that the crowd greeted Jesus on his entry into Jerusalem: 'This is the prophet Jesus from Nazareth in Galilee' (Matthew 21.11). And he goes on to record that the chief priests and Pharisees hesitated to arrest Jesus during his final week in Jerusalem: 'they feared the crowds, because they regarded him as a prophet' (21.46). Earlier in his career, the Synoptic Evangelists all narrate the story of Jesus teaching in the synagogue at Nazareth and responding to the offence taken by the congregation by commenting that 'A prophet is not without honour, except in his own country . . .' (Mark 6.4). According to Mark one of the earlier opinions considered by King Herod was that Jesus was a prophet, 'like one of the prophets of old' (Mark 6.15). And Luke records a similar response to one of his miracles: 'A great prophet has risen among us' (Luke 7.16). Later on, he has Jesus affirming that he must go to Jerusalem, despite threats to his life, 'because it is impossible for a prophet to be killed outside of Jerusalem' (13.33). And rather poignantly he records two of Jesus' disciples, before they had heard of Jesus' resurrection, explaining sadly to a stranger (the risen Jesus!) that they were unhappy because Jesus of Nazareth, 'a prophet mighty in deed and word' had been executed (24.19).

Interestingly, John 's Gospel also gives some prominence to the expectation regarding 'the prophet' (John 1.21–25) and to the crowd's speculation that Jesus fulfilled this role

(6.14; 7.40; 9.17). And in Acts there is no hesitation in presenting Jesus as the eschatological[3] prophet predicted by Moses for the final stage of history (Acts 3.22–23; 7.37). That no more is made of this assessment of Jesus in the rest of the New Testament presumably implies that this was an early view of Christ, rooted in claims made by Jesus regarding his ministry, but superseded by further assessments of his significance.

A teacher

It is well worth noting how often Jesus was referred to as 'teacher' during his ministry.[4] All the more striking is the fact that he was not so remembered in the NT outside the Gospels. This can only mean that Jesus was known and often spoken about during his mission as a teacher. It is of some interest, then, that the Jesus tradition has been allowed to retain this – a feature which strengthens the impression that the Synoptic tradition derives primarily from the historical memory of the first disciples. Equally of interest is the fact that the use of 'teacher' in the Gospels mirrors the predominance of parables as characteristic of Jesus' teaching despite the relative absence of parable as a teaching form thereafter. The retention of both features is a reminder of how strong was the impact made by Jesus' teaching on those who came to see him in much more exalted terms.

Anointed with God's Spirit

As we saw in Chapter 2, the Gospel writers all recall the Baptist's prediction that as he baptized with water, so Jesus would baptize with the Holy Spirit. They also affirm that

Jesus' baptism was immediately followed or completed by the Spirit coming upon him (Mark 1.10) and that his time in the wilderness after his baptism was at the Spirit's instigation (1.12). Otherwise Mark only has Jesus warning against blaspheming the Spirit (3.29) and promising his disciples that in times of trial they would be inspired by the Holy Spirit in their speech (13.11). In turn, Matthew explicitly attributes Jesus' conception to the Holy Spirit (Matthew 1.18, 20) – clearly indicating that the story of Jesus and the Spirit did not start at the Jordan. Like Mark, he has Jesus promising his disciples that in times of trial it would be given to them what to say, for it would be the Spirit speaking through them (10.19–20). Unique to Matthew, however, is his citation of Isaiah 42.1–4 as fulfilled in Jesus: 'I will put my Spirit upon him, and he will proclaim justice to the Gentiles' (Matthew 12.18). And he follows that up by narrating how Jesus attributed his success as an exorcist to the Spirit (12.28), and warning his critics not to blaspheme against the Spirit by malicious criticism of his exorcisms (12.31–32/ Luke 12.10).

Luke begins his Gospel by describing the predictor of Jesus' role to be baptizer in the Holy Spirit as himself filled with the Spirit from birth.[5] That is, he does not hesitate to use language typical of the earliest church ('full of the Spirit', 'filled with the Spirit') for the beginning of his history of Jesus. Luke also has Jesus himself early on laying claim to be the eschatological prophet anointed by the Spirit to bring his message of good news, as promised by Isaiah 61.1–2 (Luke 4.17–21). Nor does he hesitate to depict Jesus as rejoicing in the Holy Spirit (10.21) and as promising that the heavenly Father would give the Holy Spirit to those who ask him (11.13).

In turn, the Fourth Evangelist develops the earlier teaching on the Spirit, showing just how important it had become and how important it was to attribute the Spirit to Jesus. Thus he elaborates the Baptist's testimony to Jesus anointed by the Spirit (John 1.32–33), depicts Jesus as instructing Nicodemus on being born of the Spirit (3.3–8), and rounds off his testimony to the Baptist by attesting that Jesus 'gives the Spirit without measure' (3.34). He has Jesus warning not to put too much emphasis on the eucharistic bread, since 'it is the Spirit that gives life' (6.63), depicting the Spirit as living water to be drunk (7.38–39; cf. 4.14), characterizing the Spirit as 'the Spirit of truth' (14.17; 15.26; 16.13), and even as anticipating the Pentecostal gift of the Spirit (20.22). All this may tell us too little about Jesus' actual teaching on the Spirit of God. But it certainly confirms how central to the earliest Christian memory of Jesus was his own Spirit commissioning and his promise that the Spirit would be given to his disciples.

Messiah

That Jesus thus anointed was Israel's long-expected Messiah (= Christ in Greek) was fundamental for the first Christians. The Synoptic Gospels build up the claim slowly: first hailed as such by demoniacs (Mark 1.24; 3.11), confessed by Peter (8.29) and climactically condemned by Pilate as 'king of the Jews' (15.9–26). Because such a claim was liable to be misunderstood, in terms of political leadership, Mark shows Jesus keeping the claim quiet (1.25; 3.12), until he could explain that Messiahship meant suffering and death, but also resurrection (8.31; 9.31; 10.33–34). John's retelling of the story of Jesus' mission, in contrast, showed no such inhibition (John 1.41; 4.25–26, 29). The claim became so fundamental for the first Christians that the title (the Messiah) became part of Jesus' proper name (Jesus Christ). That believers were 'in Christ' became a basic assumption of Paul.

The Son of Man

Somewhat controversially, Jesus is remembered as often referring to himself as 'the Son of Man'. Since the phrase appears regularly in the Jesus tradition, and hardly at all outside,[6] use of it can certainly be attributed to Jesus himself. Of all the self-reference language used by Jesus, this is the most intriguing. Intriguing because it is simply an Aramaic idiom denoting the human person's human origin – as in Psalm 8.4. But also because in a vision recorded in Daniel 7.13–14, the phrase was used of a human figure 'coming with the clouds of heaven' (in contrast to the Ancient of Days), one to whom was given universal dominion.

In Jesus' usage the phrase often seems to function as equivalent to 'a man like me' – in claiming authority to pronounce forgiveness of sins (Mark 2.10), in justifying apparent disregard of the Sabbath laws (2.27–28), in diminishing the seriousness of words spoken against him (3.28–29), in referring to his sense of being disowned (Matthew 8.20/Luke 9.58), and in contrasting himself with John the Baptist (Matthew 11.18–19/Luke 7.33–34). In several cases where one Evangelist has Jesus speaking of the Son of Man, another uses 'I'/'me' in the same saying[7] – presumably a sure confirmation that Jesus was recalled as using the phrase in self-reference.

On other occasions the influence of Daniel 7.13 is evident – when Jesus is recorded as predicting that his hearers would see the Son of Man 'coming in clouds' with power.[8] Most intriguing is the fact that Jesus is recalled as using the same phrase in self-reference when anticipating his betrayal and execution,[9] but also of his expectation of future vindication (Mark 8.38; 9.9).

From all this the most obvious conclusions to draw are (1) that Jesus used the phrase regularly in self-reference;

and (2) that he drew on Daniel's vision to express his evident sense of destiny, both as to his likely death, but if so, also of his expectation that the final outcome would include his vindication. It is somewhat surprising that the earliest churches did not make more of the phrase, especially as in itself it would enable them to embrace the thought of Jesus' everyday humanity and his crucial role from a heavenly perspective. But the very fact that they did not do so strengthens the historian's confidence that this must have been one of Jesus' preferred self-references.

Son of God

That Jesus was/is God's son, and uniquely so, is of course a fundamental element of Christian faith. It is obvious from the great Christian confessions that the understanding of Jesus as God's son was greatly developed or more sharply defined during the first three centuries of Christianity. It is equally evident from the New Testament Gospels that Jesus' reference to God as Father has been considerably expanded.[10] It would also appear that the first believers did not hesitate to speak of Jesus in terms of Psalm 2.7, 'You are my son; today I have begotten you'[11] – perhaps using words previously spoken in regard to the king when he ascended the throne. That this belief was rooted in earliest traditions regarding Jesus is again suggested by the words which are central to the accounts of Jesus' baptism, where Jesus is addressed: 'You are my Son, the Beloved' (Mark 1.11). Intriguing is the Lukan variant (Luke 3.22), with its complete quotation of Psalm 2.7. Was it a reflection on the significance of the event, or suppressed as giving too much credence to the thought of Jesus having been adopted as God's son? Equally interesting is the fact that Matthew and Luke depict the subsequent temptations of Jesus as basically a questioning of Jesus' sense of sonship – 'If you are the Son of God . . .' (Matthew 4.3, 6/Luke 4.3, 9).

Somewhat surprisingly – surprising in the light of the subsequent importance of the conviction that Jesus was uniquely God's son – the early references to Jesus as God's son are limited. Of interest is the fact that the first to hail Jesus as 'Son of God' were apparently demoniacs[12] – insights withheld from normal view? Only at his trial and execution is the question posed explicitly – 'Are you the Messiah, the Son of the Blessed One?' (Mark 14.61). And Mark rounds off his account of Jesus' death on the cross with the Roman centurion's confession, 'Truly this man was God's Son' (15.39). Given the subsequent importance of and emphasis on the claim that Jesus was God's Son, the minimal focus on it by the first Evangelists has the greater credibility.

Even more surprising is the fact that Jesus was remembered as praying to God as 'Abba (Father)'. The word is a rather intimate family word, equivalent to the nineteenth-century 'Papa' and the twentieth-century 'Dad' or even 'Daddy'. The first Christians clearly relished the thought that they could so pray to God and saw it as attesting their having been given to share in Jesus' own relation with God.[13] It is of interest, then, that although Jesus is recalled as regularly speaking of God as 'Father', only once is he remembered as addressing God as 'Abba' – significantly, in the trauma of Gethsemane (Mark 14.36). On the other hand, there is no reason to doubt Luke's repeated references to Jesus' own prayer life, with the clear corollary that his sense of sonship was expressed regularly in his prayers.

5

Conclusion

One of the remarkable features of the Synoptic Gospel traditions regarding Jesus is how clear and how firm is the picture they retained and depict of Jesus. In comparison with the Fourth Gospel, and later would-be Gospels, the Synoptic account is remarkably consistent and coherent – the impact made by Jesus well conveyed by the clear memories (same or similar) of what he said and did.

Several elements in the biography are clear beyond reasonable dispute: in particular, that Jesus was a native of Nazareth, was baptized in the river Jordan by the Baptist, and focused his ministry largely in Galilee. A striking feature is how faithful were the memories of Jesus' ministry, even when characteristic features of his ministry did not carry over into the early church's own message. In particular it is very noticeable that Jesus was remembered as speaking much of the kingdom of God, and as giving his teaching a distinctive and penetrating force by narrating memorable episodes and stories (parables). More fully carried over into the earliest Christian mission were his powerful ministry of exorcism and healing, the priority he gave to the poor and his insistence that his good news was primarily for the sinner.

When Jesus' mission and commission were summed up they included the portrayal of Jesus as a prophet and a teacher, even though such categories were left behind as early Christian assessment of Jesus developed. That he had been anointed by God's Spirit was retained in what became the standard reference to him as the 'Christ', God's anointed one. His regular self-reference as 'the Son of Man' was also retained in the memories of Jesus contained in the Gospels, even though the title hardly featured in the earliest church's own theological reflection on his significance. Above all, the conviction that Jesus was God's Son, and that his sonship was distinctive from early believers' sonship, which was understood to be derived from it, was deeply rooted in the earliest memories of Jesus' experience at Jordan and of Jesus' prayer life.

There need be little doubt, then, that the Synoptic accounts of Jesus are deeply rooted in and well represent the impression and impact which Jesus actually made on his first disciples.

Notes

1 Introduction

1 'Evangelist' is the usual way of denoting the writer of each Gospel (the archaic word for 'gospel' is 'evangel').

2 Next to the Temple priests in Jerusalem the Pharisees were the most influential sect within first-century Judaism.

2 Jesus' life

1 Matthew 13.55; Mark 6.3; Acts 1.14.

2 James in particular became a leading figure in earliest Christianity (Acts 12.17; 15.13; 21.18; 1 Corinthians 15.7; Galatians 1.19; 2.9, 12; James 1.1).

3 He could equally be referred to as 'Jesus the Galilean' (Matthew 26.69).

4 The Holy Spirit was understood as the immediate presence of God.

5 'Messiah' is the usual designation of the one whom most Jews hoped would deliver Israel from Roman domination.

6 Mark 3.19; Matthew 26.25; Luke 22.48.

7 This council was the nearest to self-government that the Roman rulers would allow.

8 John 19.36; Exodus 12.10, 46.

3 Jesus' mission

1 Mark 8.35; 10.29; 13.10.

2 Psalms 10.16; 22.28; 29.10; 47.2, 7–8, 95.3; 103.19; 135.6.

3 Psalms 93.1–2; 96.10; 97.1; 99.1.

4 Acts 14.22; 19.8b; 20.25 – indeed, it brackets his whole account (1.3; 28.31).

5 Exodus 22.25–27; 23.11; Leviticus 19.10; 23.22; Deuteronomy 15.11; 24.14–15.

6 Romans 15.26; 2 Corinthians 8–9; Galatians 2.10; James 2.1–7.

7 Isaiah 29.18; 35.6; 42.7, 18.

8 Mark 1.23–28, 32–34, 39; 3.11.

9 Mark 8.22–26; 10.46–52; Matthew 9.27–31.

10 Mark 1.29–31; 7.31–37; Luke 14.1–6; 22.50–51.

11 E.g. Romans 15.19; 1 Corinthians 12.9, 30.

12 Acts 3.6; 4.10, 30; 16.18; cf. Matthew 7.22; Mark 9.39; Luke 10.17; Acts 19.13.

13 E.g. Numbers 32.14; Psalms 1.1, 5; 26.9; 104.35; Isaiah 1.28; Amos 9.10.

14 On Jesus as 'the Son of Man' see Chapter 4.

15 Acts 2.38; 3.19; 5.31; 10.43; 13.38–39; 26.18.

16 Romans 3.25; 1 Corinthians 15.3; 1 Peter 2.24; 3.18; 1 John 2.2.

17 Cf. Matthew 19.28/Luke 22.30.

18 'Yahweh' was Israel's special name for God, drawn from Exodus 3.14.

19 Matthew 8.11–12; 21.43; 22.8–9; 24.14; 28.19–20.

20 Matthew 8.5–13/Luke 7.2–10; Mark 7.24–30.

21 Luke 3.21; 5.16; 6.12; 9.18, 28–29; 11.1.

22 Luke 1.52; 4.18; 6.20; 14.13, 21; 16.19–31; 18.22; 19.8.

23 Luke 6.24; 12.15–21, 33; 16.19–31; 19.8–9.

24 Luke 8.2–3; 10.38–42; 18.2–5; 23.27–29.

4 Jesus' self-understanding

1 Luke 4.18, 43; 9.48; 10.16.

2 Matthew 14.5; Mark 11.32.

3 'Eschatological' indicates expectations for the *eschaton*, 'the final days'.

4 E.g. Mark 4.38; 5.35; 9.17, 38; 10.17, 20, 35, 51; 12.14, 19; 12.32; 13.1; 14.14.

5 Luke 1.15; note also 1.41, 67.

6 Acts 7.56 is the most notable exception.

7 Luke 6.22/Matthew 5.11; Luke 12.8/Matthew 10.32; Matthew 16.13/Mark 8.27; Mark 10.45/Luke 22.27.

8 Mark 13.26; 14.62; also 8.38.

9 Mark 8.31; 9.31; 10.33; 10.45; 14.21; 14.41.

10 In Mark Jesus refers to God as 'Father' three times, in Luke four, in Matthew 31 and in John 100.

11 Acts 13.33; Hebrews 1.5; 5.5.

12 Matthew 8.29; Mark 3.11/Luke 4.41.

13 Romans 8.14–17; Galatians 4.6–7.

Further reading

Barrett, C. K. *Jesus and the Gospel Tradition*. London: SPCK, 1967.

Bornkamm, G. *Jesus of Nazareth*. London: Hodder & Stoughton, 1960.

Conzelmann, H. *Jesus*. Philadelphia, PA: Fortress, 1973.

Dodd, C. H. *The Founder of Christianity*. London: Collins, 1971.

Dunn, J. D. G. *Jesus Remembered*. Grand Rapids, MI: Eerdmans, 2003.

Evans, C. A. *Jesus and his Contemporaries*. Leiden: Brill, 1995.

Harvey, A. E. *Jesus and the Constraints of History*. London: Duckworth, 1982.

McKnight, S. *A New Vision for Israel: The Teachings of Jesus in National Context*. Grand Rapids, MI: Eerdmans, 1999.

Meier, J. P. *A Marginal Jew*. 4 vols. New York: Doubleday, 1991, 1994, 2001, 2009.

Meyer, B. F. *The Aims of Jesus*. London: SCM, 1979.

O'Collins, G. *Jesus: A Portrait*. Maryknoll, NY: Orbis, 2008.

Sanders, E. P. *The Historical Figure of Jesus*. London: Penguin, 1993.

Theissen, G. *The Shadow of the Galilean: The Quest of the Historical Jesus in Narrative Form*. London: SCM, 1987.

Vermes, G. *Jesus the Jew*. London: SCM, 1993.

Wright, N. T. *Jesus and the Victory of God*. London: SPCK, 1992.